Raspberry Pi

**Essential Step by Step Beginner's Guide
with Cool Projects and Programming
Examples in Python**

George Kemper

First Edition: 06/2017
ISBN-13: 978-1974545506
ISBN-10: 1974545504

ii

Executive Summary

It is roughly five years now since the original Raspberry PI was launched. Having been launched on 29 February 2012 - which was a leap-year-day - Eben Upton and his co-inventors did not know that the Raspberry PI Foundation they were launching would leap into unknown territories.

But how could they have foreseen the impact this tiny computing module designed around an ARM processor with discrete specifications would have on the global education community? Thanks to this invention, we have witnessed phenomenal growth in Raspberry PI sales with three versions developed.

Today, Raspberry Pi is more than just a teaching tool to encourage kids to learn and enjoy programming. It is being applied across a host of industries from smartphones to IoT with impressive and unprecedented commercial success stories.

While many tech enthusiasts are ecstatic about its uses as an affordable computer, the majority of hobbyists are considering it as key to unraveling a whole world of possibilities.

Obviously, you can't paint a landscape without learning its basics. That's why we have come up with this book— to show you how to get a grip on the world's most famous credit card-sized computer. If you're a newbie, or you just want to help a friend or relative, reading this ebook will be a remarkable way to get you started.

We also know that when it comes to making and hacking, the sky is certainly not the limit; we'll also dive deeper to provide you with a big picture view of programming in Raspberry Pi.

Enjoy reading!

Table of Contents

Chapter 1:

Introduction to the

Raspberry Pi

By now, you must have come across, or probably seen mentions of, the word Raspberry Pi in your travels across the Web, but what exactly is it? What can you do with Raspberry Pi and why would you want to consider buying it?

This chapter introduces you to the ins and outs of Raspberry Pi so that you can have a complete big picture view. Are you ready?

What is the Raspberry Pi?

Raspberry Pi is just a mini-computer, such as the one inside your laptop but with a lot less computing power. You can perceive a Raspberry Pi as a miniature, credit card-sized computer inspired by the 1981 BBC Micro.

Raspberry Pi was originally designed for education purposes. Its inventor, Eben Upton, conceived it as a low-cost device to allow kids to have an affordable and light-weight device to help them hone their skills in programming and the underlying hardware.

Thanks to its small size nature and low-cost, it was quickly adopted by vendors, tinkerers and other electronic enthusiasts for launching projects that demanded more than the core micro-controller.

Today Raspberry Pi is more than just any teaching tool for encouraging kids to learn and enjoy basic hardware skills and programming. While many tech enthusiasts are ecstatic about its uses as an affordable computer, the majority of hobbyists are considering it as key to unraveling a whole world of possibilities. The majority of the projects made on a Raspberry Pi are open with proper documentation as well and are the things you can develop and modify yourself.

It is being applied across a horde of industries from smartphones to IoT with impressive, unprecedented commercial success stories. Part of the reason for this exponential growth and adoption from a wider global community is its open source nature.

The Raspberry Pi is an open hardware except for the first chip— the Broadcom SoC (System on a Chip)—that runs many of the principal components of the motherboard such as CPU, memory, graphics and the USB controller. It's not just the SoC design that makes the Raspberry Pi different from other processors you have on your desktop or laptop.

Raspberry Pi uses a different instruction set architecture (ISA), commonly known as ARM. Developed by Acorn Computers in the late 1980s, ARM architecture is a relatively unexceptional sight in the desktop computing world. It excels in mobile devices such as your smartphone that has certainly at least one ARM-based processing core.

The ARM's combination of a simple reduced instruction set (RISC) architecture and the low power consumption makes it the perfect choice over the desktop chips that have high energy consumption rates and complex instruction set (CISC) architectures. In fact, the ARM-based BCM2835 processor is the main secret behind the Raspberry Pi abilities to operate on just 5V and 1A power supply provided by the onboard micro-USB port.

It's also the main reason why you will not find any heat-sinks on the device since the chip's low power consumption directly translates into petite waste heat, even when performing complicated processing tasks.

The fact that Raspberry Pi is ARM-based means that it is not compatible with traditional PC software. The majority of software for desktops that have inbuilt x86 instruction set architectures are based on either AMD, Intel or VIA and, therefore, these apps won't run on Raspberry Pi.

Raspberry Pi Models

There are currently three Raspberry models namely: Raspberry Pi (original), Raspberry Pi 2 and Raspberry Pi 3. The Raspberry Pi3 is the third generation of Raspberry Pi. It replaced Raspberry Pi 2 Model B in February 2016.

Compared to Raspberry Pi 2, Raspberry Pi3 has the following features:
- 1.2GHz 64-bit quad-core ARMv8 CPU
- 802.11n Wireless LAN
- Bluetooth 4.1
- BLE (Bluetooth Low Energy)
- Just like Raspberry Pi 2, Raspberry Pi 3 also has:
- 1GB of RAM
- 4 USB ports

- 40 GPIO pins
- A Full HDMI port
- An Ethernet port
- Combined 3.5millimeter audio jack and composite video
- Camera interface (CSI)
- Display interface (DSI)
- Micro SD card slot that is now a push-pull rather than the push-push)
- Video Core IV 3D graphics core

The Raspberry Pi 3 has a similar form factor to the previous models (Raspberry Pi 2 and Pi 1 type B+). It is also compatible with Raspberry Pi 1 and Pi 2.

If you intend to buy a Raspberry for use in schools or any general use, we recommend Raspberry Pi 3 Model B. However, if you wish to embed your Pi in a project, you can consider Raspberry Pi Zero or Model A+ which are more helpful for embedded projects.

Raspberry OS

The majority of desktop computing systems available today run one of the two popular operating systems: Microsoft Windows or Apple OS X. These platforms are closed source, meaning they have been developed in a secretive environment using proprietary techniques.

Being closed source platforms also means that their source codes are closely-guarded and you can only obtain the finished software and can't see how it has been coded.

The Raspberry Pi, by contrast, is conceived to operate on GNU/Linux OS that we'll just call Linux. Unlike the Windows or OS X, Linux is open source. Therefore, it is possible to download the source code for the complete OS and make it do whatever changes you desire.

In Linux, nothing is hidden. Therefore, all the changes you make will be in full view of the public. This open source development ethos has enabled Linux to be easily altered to run on the Raspberry Pi through a process commonly called porting. At the time of writing this book, many versions of Linux—called distributions—had already been ported to the

Raspberry Pi's ARM chip. These include Debian, Fedora Remix, and the Arch Linux. These different distributions cater to various user needs, but they all have one thing in common: they are open source.

They are also all, generally, compatible with one another. For instance, software written on a Debian-based system will seamlessly operate on a Fedora-based Linux distribution and vice-versa. But Linux isn't just exclusive to the Raspberry Pi. Today, there are hundreds of different distributions available for desktops, laptops and even mobile devices.

Recall that Google's popular Android OS platform is developed on top of the Linux core. Therefore, if you enjoy the experience of using Linux on Raspberry Pi, you may consider adding it to other computing devices such as Android smartphones as well. Such an environment allows you to enjoy the benefits of Raspberry Pi while providing you a familiar environment.

Today many Linux distributions have a version specifically optimized for the Raspberry Pi. Two of the most popular options are Raspbian and Pidora. As their names suggests, Raspbian is based on Debian and Pidora is based on Fedora-based Linux distributions.

If you are a beginner, either of these two platforms will work just as well. Whatever you choose is a matter of personal preference. However, a good practice might be to select the one that closely resembles the Linux distribution you are familiar with, in either a desktop or server working environment.

Now that you know what Raspberry is and the operating system you'll require, what is next? Well, let's get started.

Getting Started with the Raspberry Pi

You've just received your Raspberry Pi. What do you do with it? If you've just obtained your Raspberry Pi, the first thing to do would be to take it out of its protective bag and place it on any flat, non-conductive surface. You should ensure that the display, the audio, the keyboard and the mouse are ready and with you.

Next up, let's explore how you can connect these devices.

Connecting the Display

Even before you begin to use your Pi, you're going to need a display system. The Raspberry Pi supports three different video outputs: the composite video, the HDMI video, and the DSI video. While the composite video and HDMI video are readily available to the end user, the DSI video requires some specialized hardware.

The Composite Video

The composite video is available through the yellow-and-silver port on your Pi. To connect the display unit, you'll need an RCA phono connector. The RCA phono connector is designed to connect the Pi to older display devices. This connector will create a composite of the colors found within an image (RGB) and sends them down a single wire to the display unit which may be an old CRT.

The HDMI Video

Excellent quality images can be obtained using the HDMI connector. Unlike the analog composite connection, HDMI port offers a high-speed digital connection for improved resolution on both computer monitors and HD TV sets. If you want to use the Pi with your existing computer screen, you should ensure that you have the HDMI-to-DVI cable. The HDMI-to-DVI cable will allow you to connect your desktop monitor to the Raspberry Pi's HDMI port.

DSI Video

The final video output on the Raspberry Pi will be found above the SD card slot on the top of the PCB (printed circuit board). The DSI (Display Serial Interface) connector is a small ribbon connector protected by a layer of plastic. It is used in the flat-panel displays of tablets and smartphones. These connectors are rare. However, if you are an engineer who wants to create a compact and self-contained system, you may consider DSI connectors.

Connecting Audio

If you're using the Pi's HDMI port, connecting audio is simple. If properly configured, the HDMI port can carry both the digital audio and video signal. This means that you'll only plug in a single cable to your display device and enjoy both sound and pictures.

Supposing you're connecting the Raspberry Pi to a standard HDMI display, then there's little to do at this point. For now, it's just enough to connect the cable.

However, if you're using the Raspberry Pi with a DVI-D monitor through the adapter or cable, audio won't be included. You'll need a black 3.5-millimeter audio jack located on the top edge of the Raspberry Pi next to the yellow phono connector. This is the same connector you'll use for headphones and microphones.

Connecting a Keyboard and Mouse

At this stage, you have your Raspberry Pi output devices—display and audio—sorted. It is now time to think about how you'll connect the input. At best, you're going to require a keyboard. And for most users, a mouse or trackball will also be necessary. If your keyboard and mouse have PS/2 connectors, I have bad news for you—go out and buy a replacement.

Raspberry Pi expects all your peripherals to be connected to the USB port. Depending on whether have Model A or Model B, you will have either one or two USB ports available on the right side. If you are using a Model B, you can connect your keyboard and mouse directly to the USB ports. If you have a Model A, you'll need to buy a USB hub that connects the two USB devices simultaneously.

As you can see, connecting peripheral devices to the Raspberry Pi is simple, isn't it? What next?

There are many other things we haven't discussed yet— the Pi's storage system, network system and power. As you've probably noted, Pi doesn't have a traditional hard disk drive. Rather, it uses a Secure Digital (SD) memory card—a solid-state storage device—such as the one employed in digital cameras. Almost any SD card will work with the Pi. But because the SD card will keep the entire OS, it must have at least 2GB capacity to store all required files.

SD cards that have OS preloaded in them are available from the official Raspberry Pi Store. You can also find these cards from numerous other websites on the Internet. If you have purchased one or received it in a bundle with your Raspberry Pi, just plug it into the SD card slot located on the bottom side of the left-hand edge. If not, you'll have to install the OS yourself. We call this process flashing. Let's dive in to explore how it is done.

Flashing the SD Card

To prepare an empty SD card for use with the Pi, you'll have to flash an OS onto the card. While this process is slightly more complicated than just dragging and dropping files onto the SD card, it shouldn't take you more than a few minutes to finish.

First, you have to decide which Linux distribution you want to use on Raspberry Pi. As mentioned earlier, there are two distributions you can opt for—Raspbian and Pidora. Each distribution has its pros and cons. At this time, don't bother if you change your mind later and want to try a new OS; you can always flash the SD card. In this book, I will use Raspbian OS for illustration purposes. However, you can also use Pidora if you wish.

The most updated list of Linux releases compatible with the Raspberry Pi are available from the Raspberry Pi official website at:
http://www.raspberrypi.org/downloads.

Both Raspbian and Pidora are provided as a single image file compressed for faster download. Once you download your compressed file (zip file), you will need to decompress it somewhere on your PC. For most OS platforms, you can just double-click the file to open it and then select "Extract" or "Unzip" to retrieve the file contents.

When you decompress the file, you will end up with two separate ones. The file that ends with a "sha1" is a hash file that can be used to verify whether the downloaded file has been corrupted or not. The second file will end with "img" and contains the exact copy of an SD card set up instructions for use on Raspberry Pi. This img file is what needs to be flashed to the SD card.

To set up Raspbian on the Pi, you will need a computer—and for that matter, a proper, functional computer—to start with. Don't worry about the OS. You can use your favorite OS to flash the SD card.

Let us see how you can flash the SD card in different OS platforms.

Flashing from Linux

If your PC is running a variant of Linux distribution already, you can use the "dd" command to help write the img file out to the SD card. The "dd" command is a text-interface program operated from the command prompt that can help you write the contents of img file quickly to the SD card.

Here are steps that can help you write the img file onto the SD card:

Step one: Launch the terminal from your Linux distribution's applications menu.

Step two: Insert your blank SD card into the card reader connected to your PC.

Step three: Now, type `sudo fdisk -l` to check the list of disks of disks attached to the PC. Locate the SD card by its size and find its device address (`/dev/sdX`, where x is a letter that identifies the storage device. Some Linux distributions can have integrated SD card readers that can handle the alternative format such as `/dev/mmcblkX`. If this is the case, then recall changing the target in the following instructions that follow accordingly.

Step four: Use the "cd "command to switch to the directory that has the ".img" file you extracted from the Zip archive.

Step Five: Type the following command: "`sudo dd if=imagefilename.img of=/dev/sdX bs=2M`" and hit the Enter key to write the file `imagefilename.img` to the SD card connected to the device address from step 3. This step will take some time, so be patient! When copying has been completed, type: "`sudo diskutil eject /dev/disk[n]`" to remove the SD card.

Step Six: Remove the SD card and plug it into your Raspberry Pi 3.

Flashing from Mac OS

Here are steps to help you set up a Raspberry Pi 3 on a Mac:

Step one: Use an appropriate SD Formatter app to format your SD Card. Remove the SD card from your Apple Mac.

Step two: Open the Safari browser and head to https://www.raspberrypi.org/downloads and download the zipped Raspbian. Ensure you have selected the full version and not Raspbian Jessie Lit.

Step three: Double-click the downloaded Raspbian zipped file in your Downloads folder to extract your image file.

Step Four: Launch the Terminal.

Step Five: Enter the following command at the command prompt: "`diskutil list`." You will now see a list of all your drives. If you have a Mac with just one hard disk, two drives will appear: the "/dev/disk0" and "/dev/disk1." If you have several external hard drives, there will be more drives.

Step six: Now attach your SD Card to the Mac.

Step Seven: Type "disktuil list" again. Check carefully to ensure you can locate the new SD card. Check to make sure its size matches the SD Card. It is important you get this step right so that you don't end up overwriting data on a wrong drive.

Step eight: Type "sudo diskutil unmountDisk /dev/disk[n]" (replace with the correct number of the disk such as /dev/disk2).

Step nine: Now type "sudo dd bs=1m if=~/Downloads/2016-03-18-raspbian-jessie.img of=/dev/rdisk[n]" (you should replace [n] with the number of the disk to write the contents of the img file to the SD card). When copying has been completed, type: "sudo diskutil eject /dev/disk[n]" to eject the SD card.

Step Ten: Remove the SD card and plug it into your Raspberry Pi 3.

Flashing from Windows

The process of flashing the SD card on Windows is a bit more straightforward. You will need to download the "Win32 Disk Imager" app that can be obtained from SourceForge. Here are steps that can help you flash the SD card in Windows:

Step one: Download the Win32 Disk Imager" app from SourceForge and install it on your PC.

Step two: Run Win32 Disk Imager as an administrator by right-clicking the program icon and selecting "Run as administrator."

Step three: Choose the image file you extracted from the Raspbian Zipped file.

Step four: Choose the correct SD card by selecting the drive letter in the drop-down menu below the "Device." Be completely sure that you have selected the correct drive before proceeding.

Step five: Now click "Write." This process will take some time to complete. However, when the process terminates, you can eject the device and plug it into the Raspberry Pi.

We have now successfully flashed the SD card, meaning we have the Raspberry OS (Raspbian) on our Pi. What next? Obviously, you'll need to connect to the network and access Internet services. You can either set up a wired network or a wireless network.

Setting up Wired Networking

To get your Raspberry Pi on the wired network, you'll need to connect the RJ45 Ethernet patch cable between the Pi and your LAN switch or router. If you don't have either a router or hub, you can connect your desktop or laptop to the Pi by joining the two directly together with a patch cable.

Contemporary Raspberry Pi models don't provide any form of wireless network capability onboard. However, by adding wired Ethernet to the Model A, you can add Wi-Fi support to any Raspberry Pi using a USB wireless adapter.

Connecting Power

At this stage, you're now anxious to begin using your Raspberry Pi. Before you start to experiment with it, it is important to learn how to power it. The Raspberry Pi is powered by using the small micro-USB connector found on the lower left side of the motherboard. This powering connector is the same one found on the majority of smartphones and other tablet devices.

Many chargers designed for smartphones will work just fine with the Raspberry Pi, but not all. The Raspberry Pi is more power-hungry than most micro-USB devices and will require up to 700mA to operate optimally.

Chapter 2: Basic Linux Administration Skills

Both Raspbian and Pidora are free OS's based on Debian and Fedora Linux distributions respectively. These platforms have been optimized for the Raspberry Pi hardware. As with the majority of contemporary Linux distributions, both Raspbian and Pidora are free and open source and bundled with many packages in a nice format for easy installations on any Pi.

However, if you are used to either Windows or Mac OS, you'll get the most out of your Raspberry Pi because these systems aren't based on the Linux kernel. This is why you'll need a quick primer into basic Linux administration skills. Are you ready?

An overview of Linux OS

An operating system is just a set of basic programs and utilities that can make your PC run efficiently. Linux is an open source system originally conceived to produce a kernel—the core and heart of any OS that manages communication between users and hardware—it would be free for any individual to use.

Being an OS, Linux OS will handle mundane functions such as process management, memory management, file system management and hardware devices. Therefore, any Linux administrator should have the basic skills of how it can handle these tasks. Since Raspbian is a Linux OS, it means that managing the Raspberry Pi will involve understanding how activities such as process management, memory management, file system management and hardware devices are managed.

Even though it is only the kernel that qualifies to be called the Linux, the term has continued to be used to refer to collections of different open source systems from a variety of vendors. These groups come together forming different flavors of Linux; they are collectively known as distributions.

The original Linux version was combined with a collection of tools created by a group called GNU. The resulting platform, called GNU/Linux, was basic but very powerful. Unlike other OS's of that era, it provided facilities such as multiple user accounts where many users could share a single computer.

This is something that other rival closed-source operating systems began to take on board with both Windows and OS X now supporting many user accounts on the same system. These features are still present in modern Linux distributions and provide security for the operating system.

Linux users spend most of their time running a restricted user account. This doesn't mean that they are limited to what they can do. Rather, Linux prevents users from accidentally doing something that can break the software in the system. It also prevents malicious apps such as viruses and other malware from your PC by locking down access to necessary system files and directories.

Before you get started with Linux, it's vital to become familiar with some of the terminologies and concepts used. Here are standard terms employed in Linux:

- The Terminal and the GUI. There are two main ways to achieve a given task in Linux—using the graphical user interface (GUI) and the command-line. The command line—also called the Linux parlance—is offered by a Terminal or Console.

- Bash. The most popular shell choice used in the majority of Linux systems.

- Bootloader. The software responsible for loading the Linux kernel with the most common being the GRUB.

- Console. The version of the terminal app always available, and the first thing you will see on the Raspberry Pi.

- Desktop environment. The software that makes the GUI look pretty. GNOME and KDE are renowned.

- Directory. The Linux term that denotes what Windows calls folders where the files are stored.

- Distribution. A particular version of Linux such as Fedora Remix, Arch, and Debian.

- Executable. A file that can run as a program. The Linux files must be marked as executable for them to run.

- EXT2/3/4. The EXTended file system that is the most common format used in Linux.

- File system. The way the hard drive or any other storage device is formatted so that it can be ready for file storage.

- GNOME. One of the most renowned Linux desktop environments around.

- GNU. A free software project that provides many tools used in Linux distributions.

- GRUB. The GRand Unified Bootloader created by GNU and used to load the Linux kernel.

- GUI. A graphical user interface with which the user operates the computer using a mouse or touch.

- KDE. Another favorite Linux desktop environment.

- Live CD. A Linux distribution provided as a CD or DVD that doesn't require installation.

- Package. A collection of files needed to run an application, which is handled by the package manager.

- Package manager. A tool used for keeping track of and installing new software.

- Partition. A section of the hard drive ready to have a file system applied to it for storage.

- Root. The main user account in Linux equivalent to the Windows administrator account.

- Shell. A text-based command prompt loaded in a terminal.

- Sudo. A program that allows limited users to run a command as the root user.

- Terminal. A text-based command prompt where the user interacts with a shell program.

Basic Linux Commands

Even though there are hundreds of different Linux distributions available, they all share a common set of tools. These tools, which are operated using the terminal, are analogous to similar tools on Windows and Mac OS. To get you started, let us explore a few.

- `ls` (short for listing). ls generates a list of contents of the current directory. Alternatively, it can be called with an argument of the directory. As an example, when you type `ls /home` the command will generate a list of the contents of the /home directory, regardless of your current directory. The Windows equivalent is the `dir`.

- `cd` (change directory). `cd` allows you to navigate your way in the file system. Typing `cd` at the command prompt puts you back in your home directory. Typing the command with the name of the directory to which you want to move, by contrast, will switch to that directory. Note that the directories can be absolute or relative. For instance, `cd boot` will move you to the directory called `boot` under your current directory.

However, `cd /boot` moves you straight to the `/boot` directory irrespective of where you are.

- `mv` (move command). This command has two purposes in Linux: it allows a file to be moved from one folder to another and it also allows files to be renamed.

- `rm` (remove). `rm` deletes files. Any file provided with the command name will be erased. The Windows equivalent is the `del` command, and the two share a common requirement that care be taken to ensure the right file is the one deleted.

- `rmdir`(remove directory).By itself, the `rm` can't delete directories. As a result, the `rmdir` is provided to help delete folders once they have been emptied of files by the `rm` command.

- `mkdir` (the opposite of the rmdir). The `mkdir` command creates new directories. For example, typing mkdir Steve at the terminal will create a new directory called Steve under the current working directory. As with the `cd` command, the directories provided to the command can be relative or absolute.

The list of Linux commands described above are not exhaustive. You can learn more about Linux command by visiting the following URLs:

1. http://linuxcommand.org/

2. http://linuxcommand.org/learning_the_shell.php

3. http://searchenterpriselinux.techtarget.com/tutor ial/77-useful-Linux-commands-and-utilities

4. http://www.dummies.com/computers/operating- systems/linux/common-linux-commands/

Debian and Raspbian

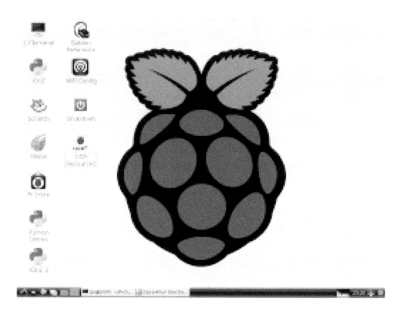

Debian-based Linux is one of the oldest Linux distributions, and an excellent choice for the Raspberry Pi, thanks to its light-weight nature. This is why the Raspberry Pi Foundation chose it to be the recommended software for beginners and the one that I am using in this book. To keep the download size to a bare minimum, the Raspberry Pi image for Debian will include only a subset of the software you would find on a regular desktop version.

These may include tools for browsing the Internet, programming in Python, and using the Raspberry Pi with a GUI. Any additional software can be easily installed through the utilization of the distribution's package manager `apt`.

The Raspberry Pi build of the Debian has a desktop environment commonly known as Lightweight X11 Desktop Environment (LXDE). LXDE is designed to provide an attractive user interface using the X Window System software. In particular, the LXDE provides a click interface immediately accessible to anyone who has used Windows, OS X or other GUI-based OS skills.

The GUI doesn't load automatically in most Raspberry Pi distributions. To quickly launch it and leave the text-based console behind, log in to your Pi and type the command: "`startx`" and then hit the Enter key. If you're using the recommended Debian-based distributions, you'll find that you have many preinstalled software to get you started.

While hardly an in-depth example of the software available for the Raspberry Pi, which numbers in the thousands of packages, it's a good practice to precisely understand what the system can do. The software provided with the Debian-based distribution is grouped into themed categories that include:

#1: Accessories

The apps falling under Accessories are:

- Debian Reference. It is a built-in reference guide that gives a detailed explanation of the Debian Linux distribution and how developers can contribute to its growth.

- File Manager. The PCManFM file manager offers a graphical browser for the files stored on the Raspberry Pi or any connected storage device.

- Image Viewer. The GPicView allows you to view images such as those from digital cameras or any connected storage device.

- Leafpad. This is a simple text editor useful for making quick notes and writing simple programs.

- LXTerminal. This is an LXDE terminal package that allows you to use the Linux command line in a window without leaving the GUI.

- Root Terminal. It is similar to the LXTerminal. However, the Root Terminal automatically logs you in as the root to perform system maintenance tasks unavailable to a regular user account.

- Xarchiver. If you want to create or extract compressed files such as ZIP archives, you can use the Xarchiver.

#2: Education

The apps that fall under Education are:

- Scratch. It is a graphical programming language aimed at young children.

- Squeak. It is the platform on which the Scratch runs.

#3: The Internet

The apps that fall under the Internet are:

- Midori. A fast yet lightweight Web browser equivalent to Internet Explorer in Windows or Safari in OS X.

- Midori Private Browsing. When you click this menu entry, you'll load the Midori Web browser in private mode meaning that sites you visit will not be saved in the browser's history.

- NetSurf Web Browser. It is an alternative to the Midori that can perform better on certain kinds of Internet pages. Trying both will enable you to experiment and find out the one that works best for you.

#4: Programming

The apps that fall under Programming are:

- IDLE. It is an integrated development environment (IDE) written specifically for Python.

- IDLE 3. Clicking this option loads the IDLE configured to use the newer version of Python (Python 3) instead of the default Python 2.7 language. Both versions are mostly compatible with each other. However, some programs may demand features of Python 3.

- Scratch. It opens the Scratch educational language and it is the same as the Scratch entry found in the Education category. Either of them can be used to start the program.

- Squeak. As with the Scratch, this is a duplicate of the shortcut found in the Education category. You will rarely want to use this shortcut directly, and are likely to prefer the Scratch shortcut.

#5: Sound & Video

The apps that fall under Sound & Video are:

- Music Player. LXMusic is a straightforward and lightweight interface to the XMMS2 music playback system that allows you to listen to music files on your Raspberry Pi.

#6: System Tools

The apps that fall under System Tools are:

- Task Manager. It is a toolkit you can use to check the amount of free memory available on the Raspberry Pi, the current workload of the processor and for closing unresponsive programs.

#7: Preferences

The apps that fall under System Tools are:

- Customize Look and Feel. It is a toolkit for tweaking the appearance of the GUI such as the style and color of the windows.

- Desktop Session Settings. It is a tool for changing how the system works after the user has logged in, including the programs that will automatically be loaded and which window manager will be used.

- Keyboard and Mouse. It is a toolkit for adjusting your input devices.

- Monitor Settings. The resolution of the monitor or the TV connected to the Raspberry Pi can be altered using the monitor settings.

- Openbox Configuration Manager. The LXDE GUI uses a desktop environment called Openbox. The GUI can be adjusted using the Openbox Configuration Manager.

- Preferred Applications. It is a toolkit for changing which apps are opened for particular file types. If you choose to use an alternative Web browser, then the system default can be changed using the Preferred Applications.

Finding Help

Linux has been designed to be as user-friendly as possible to beginners, even at the console command prompt. Even though you will learn the most common commands that you can use in the Terminal; the list isn't exhaustive. If you find yourself stuck with a particular command, or if you just want to learn more about any of the tools we have discussed, then you can use the following command at the Terminal's command prompt:

```
man
```

Every Linux distribution comes with its own help file, known as the man page or short for "manual page." The man page provides background on the software as well as the details on the options performed and how to use them.

To access the man page for a particular tool, just type man followed by the name of the command. For instance, to see the man page for the `ls` command, just type `man ls`.

How to use External Storage Devices on Raspberry Pi

The Raspberry Pi's SD card, which stores all the different Pi files and directories, isn't so big. If you're using your Raspberry Pi to play back video files, you'll likely require more storage than what you can get from your typical SD card. Fortunately, Raspberry Pi provides a way of getting around this problem.

However, before any external devices can be made accessible, the Raspberry Pi needs to know about them in advance. In Linux, we call this process *mounting*. If you're running a version of Linux that has a desktop environment already loaded such as the LXDE, then this will be automatic. Just connect the external storage device to the free USB port on the Raspberry Pi or the USB hub and the device contents will be immediately accessible.

What about if you're using a console instead of a desktop environment?

To make an external storage device accessible to Raspberry Pi when the desktop environment isn't loaded, follow these steps:

Connect the external storage device to the Pi, either directly or using a connected USB hub.

- Launch the Terminal and type "sudo fdisk –l" at the command prompt to get a list of all drives attached to the Pi. Find the USB mass storage device by size. Note the device name: "/dev/sdXN" where X is the drive letter while N is the partition number. If the mass storage device is the only device connected to the Pi, this will be `"/dev/sda1."`

- Before the USB mass storage device is accessible, Raspberry needs a mount point for it. Create the mount point by typing the following the following command:

  `sudo mkdir /media/externaldrive`

- Currently, the mass storage device is only accessible to the root user. To make it available to all the users, type the following command as a single line:

  `sudo chgrp -R users /media/externaldrive && sudo chmod -R g+w /media/externaldrive`

  and press the Enter key.

- Now, mount the USB mass storage device by typing this command:

  `sudo mount /dev/sdXN /media/externaldrive -o=rw`

  to help you access to the device and its contents.

Creating a New User Account

Unlike Windows and Mac OS, primarily created for use by a single individual, Linux is at the heart of a social operating system designed to accommodate many users. By default, Raspbian is configured with two user accounts: pi which is the normal user account and root, a superuser account with additional privileges.

Don't be tempted to log in as root all the time. Using a non-privileged user account such as pi protects you against accidentally wrecking your OS and from the problems of viruses and other malware downloaded from the Web. While it's certainly possible for you to use only the pi account, it's a good practice to create your own dedicated user account.

Further user accounts can also be set up for any friends or relatives who might want to use the Raspberry Pi. Creating a new user account on the Raspberry Pi is straightforward. Here are steps to follow:

- Log in to the Raspberry using the existing user account (user name=pi and password=raspberry) if you're using the recommended Debian distribution.

- Launch the Terminal and type the command as a single line:
  ```
  sudo useradd -m -G steve, dialout, cdrom, audio,
  plugdev,users,              lpadmin,sambashare,
  vchiq,powerdev username
  ```
  This will create a new and blank user account

called steve. Also, note that the command should be typed on a single line without spaces after the commas.

- To set a password for the new account (steve), type the following command: "sudo passwd steve" followed by the new password when prompted.

File System in Raspberry Pi

The content of the SD card is called its file system, and this content is split into multiple sections with each performing a particular function. Although it is not necessary for you to learn what each section does to use the Raspberry Pi, it is important to have a background knowledge of the file system just in case something goes wrong.

The way Linux deals with its drives, files, directories, and devices is somewhat different from other OS's such as Windows and Macs. Rather than having multiple drives labeled with letters, everything in Linux appears as a branch beneath what is called the root folder denoted by a forward slash "/". For instance, if you log into the Raspberry Pi and type "`ls /`" you'll see different directories displayed. Some of these are areas of your SD card for storing files while others are virtual directories for accessing various portions of the OS or hardware.

The directories visible in the default Debian distribution are:

- boot. It contains the Linux kernel and other package files needed to start the Raspberry Pi.

- bin. It contains OS-related binary files required to run the GUI.

- dev. It is a virtual directory that doesn't exist on the SD card. All the devices that will be connected to the system such as mass storage devices, the sound card, and the HDMI port can be accessed from here.

- etc. It stores the miscellaneous configuration files such as the list of users and their encrypted passwords.

- home. Every user gets a subdirectory beneath the home directory to store all their personal files.

- lib. This is a storage space for libraries that are shared bits of code required by numerous different apps.

- lost+found. It is a special directory where file fragments are kept if the system crashes.

- Media. It is a unique directory for removable storage devices such as USB memory sticks or external CD drives.

- mnt. This folder is used to manually mount the mass storage devices such as external hard drives.

- opt. It stores the optional software not part of the OS itself. When you install new software on Raspberry Pi, it will go here.

- proc. It is another virtual directory that contains information about running programs known in Linux as processes.

- SELinux. Files related to Security Enhanced Linux—a suite of security utilities originally built by the US National Security Agency--are stored here.

- sbin. It stores special binary files primarily used by the root account for system maintenance.

- sys. This folder is where the special operating system files are stored.

- tmp. Temporary files are kept here automatically.

- usr. This directory provides storage for user-accessible programs.

- var. This is a virtual directory that applications use to store the changing values or variables.

Installing and Uninstalling Software

The default software installed with Raspbian is enough to get you started. However, chances are you'll want to want to customize your Pi according to your own specifications. Installing a new software onto the Raspberry Pi is straightforward.

The Debian-based Linux distribution includes a toolkit called `apt`, which is a powerful package manager for installing and uninstalling apps in Raspberry Pi. Although apt is created to be operated from the command prompt, it's also user-friendly and easy to learn through GUIs for apt such as Synaptic Package Manager. However, Synaptic Package Manager can make your Pi bulky because of faulty memory.

To use apt to install a package such as Python, you'll just use the install command with the "apt-get" as follows:

```
sudo apt-get install python
```

Some software packages rely on other packages for them to operate. For instance, a programming language such as Python can depend on a compiler; a game engine can depend on graphics files, and so on. These files are called dependencies. Dependencies are one of the biggest justifications for using a package manager such as `apt` rather than installing software manually. If the package depends on other packages, the apt will automatically locate and install them.

To uninstall a software such as Python, simply launch the terminal and enter the following at the command prompt:

```
sudo apt-get remove python
```

In addition to installing and uninstalling software packages, apt can also be used to keep them up to date. Upgrading a package using apt ensures that you have received the latest updates, bug fixes, and even the security patches. Before trying to upgrade a software package, ensure that the apt cache is as fresh as possible by running a complete update:

```
sudo apt-get update
```

When updating software, you'll have two choices: you can either upgrade everything on the system at once or update individual programs. If you just want to keep your Raspberry updated, the former is achieved by entering the following command:

```
sudo apt-get upgrade
```

To update a single software package, just tell the apt to install it again. For instance, to install a Python upgrade, type:

```
sudo apt-get install thrust
```

If the app has already been installed, apt will treat it as an "in-place" upgrade. If you are already running the latest version of the package, apt will just inform you it can't upgrade the software and exit.

Chapter 3: Configuring Raspberry Pi

Because of its origins in embedded computing, the ARM chip at the heart of the Raspberry Pi does not have anything like the majority of PC's BIOS menu where various low-level system features can be configured. Rather, it depends on the text files that contains configuration strings. These configuration strings are loaded into the chip when the Raspberry Pi is powered on.

Even before we start taking a look at the various configuration options available in these files, a word of caution is necessary: altering these settings can at best interfere with booting and at worst physically damage your system.

Hardware Settings

The Raspberry Pi's hardware is managed by settings contained in a file called "config.txt." located in the

"/boot" directory. The "config.txt" file tells the Raspberry Pi how to set up its various inputs and outputs and at what speed the ARM chip and its connected memory modules should run.

If you're having issues with the graphics output like the image not filling the screen or spilling over the edge of the screen, config.txt is where you'll fix the problem. Usually, the file is empty or—on some Linux distributions—simply not present meaning that Raspberry Pi will work using its preset defaults. If you want to make changes and the file isn't there, just create a new text file called config.txt and fill in the settings you want to change.

The config.txt file can manage almost all aspects of the Raspberry Pi's hardware with the only exception being the CPU and the GPU sections of the ARM portion of the memory. The config.txt file will be read-only when the system first boots up. Any changes you make while the Raspberry Pi is running won't take effect until the system has been rebooted, or switched off and back on again.

In the event that the changes are unwanted, deleting the file from the /boot directory will be enough to restore the defaults once again. If the Raspberry Pi can't boot with your new settings, just eject the SD card and delete the config.txt from the boot partition on another computer and then re-insert it into the Pi and try again.

Usually, the Raspberry Pi will automatically detect the type of display connected and change its settings accordingly. Sometimes, however, this automatic detection may not work. This is often the case when a Pi from one country is connected to an older TV set from another. If you connect your Raspberry Pi to your TV and you can't see anything, you'll override these defaults.

The config.txt file can also control how Raspbian is loaded on the Raspberry Pi. Although the most typical method for controlling the loading of the Raspbian kernel is to use a separate file—called the cmdline.txt— it is also possible to use just the config.txt file. The following configuration settings can be used to control the boot process:

- disable commandline_tags. This tells the start.elf module to skip filling in memory locations past the 0x100 limit before loading the Raspbian kernel. This option should not be disabled, as doing so can cause Linux to boot incorrectly and crash.

- cmdline. This refers to command line parameters supposed to be passed to the Linux kernel to be used in place of the cmdline.txt file.

- kernel. The name of the kernel file that should be loaded. It can be used to load the emergency kernel.

- ramfsfile. The name of the initial RAM file system (RAMFS) that should be loaded. This entry should rarely be modified unless you have created a new initial file system with which to experiment.

- init_uart_baud. The speed of the serial console expressed in bits per second. The default speed is 115200bps, but lower values can improve the connection if the Raspberry Pi is used with an older hardware serial terminal.

Overclocking the Raspberry Pi

The config.txt file not only manages the graphics outputs of the Raspberry Pi's ARM processor, but it also allows you to control the chip in other ways. Specifically, it lets you to change the speed at which the chip runs, increasing its performance at the expense of the part's lifespan through a process called overclocking.

You should note that adjusting any of the Pi settings listed in this section can your Pi. For instance, changing settings that correspond to the memory, GPU or CPU voltages can set a fuse in the chip, which can invalidate the Pi's warranty even if the setting is returned to its default status before any damage is done.

The damage caused when using this configuration won't be put right by the Pi Foundation or by the seller from whom you bought your Raspberry Pi. When in doubt, don't change these settings: the performance gains through overclocking are not worth the risk.

The ARM multimedia processor at the heart of the Raspberry Pi is a system-on-chip (SoC) design split into two main parts: the graphics processor (GPU) and the central processor (CPU). In other words, the CPU controls all the day-to-day processing tasks while the GPU manages the process of drawing images on the screen in both 2D and 3D.

Using the config.txt file, you can overclock one or both parts of the ARM chip. You can also increase the speed at which the RAM module operates. Increasing the operating frequency of these components will result in a small increase in the Raspberry Pi's performance which is an increase of the GPU's clock frequency, meaning that 3D graphics will render at a faster pace, and the video will be decoded faster for smoother playback. Increasing the CPU's clock frequency will increase the overall performance of the device, as will raising the RAM's frequency.

The main reason the Pi isn't provided with higher operating speeds in the first place is related to the ARM chips' lifespan. The ARM is rated by its manufacturer (Broadcom) to run at the speed of 700MHz. Increasing the speed beyond this limit may work, but it will also have a disastrous effect on the lifespan of your chip. Unlike the desktop processors, SoC designs rarely have much space for overclocking.

Overclocking Settings

If you are willing to take the risk of breaking the Raspberry Pi—a process we call bricking in embedded devices—for the sake of a small performance increase, the following settings can help control the performance of your Raspberry Pi:

- `arm_freq`. It sets the core clock frequency of the CPU portion of the ARM chip, for a boost in performance. The default value is 700MHz.

- `gpu_freq`. It sets the clock frequency of the GPU portion of the ARM chip for an increase in graphics performance across all operations. The default value is 250MHz.

- `core_freq`. It sets the core clock frequency of the GPU, leaving other frequencies alone, to increase overall GPU performance. The default value is 250MHz.

- `h264_freq`. It sets the clock frequency of the GPU's hardware video decoder to increase playback of H.264 video data. The default value is 250MHz.

- `isp_freq`. It sets the clock frequency of the image sensor pipeline for increasing the capture rate of connected video hardware such as a camera. The default speed is 25 MHz.

- `v3d_freq`. It sets the clock frequency of the GPU's 3D rendering system, for an increase in visualization and gaming performance. The default value is 250MHz.

- `sdram_freq`. It sets the clock speed of the RAM chip on the Pi, to provide the entire system a small gain in performance. The default speed is 400MHz.

- `init_uart_clock`. It sets the default clock speed of the Universal Asynchronous Receiver/Transmitter (UART) used to manage the serial console. The default value is 3000000, which sets a speed of 3MHz. Changing this value is likely to have little impact beyond corrupting the output of the serial console.

- `init_emmc_clock`. It sets the default clock speed of the SD card controller with the default value of 80000000. This sets a speed of 80MHz. Increasing this value can increase reading and write from the SD card, but it can also lead to data corruption.

As with adjusting the display configuration, any alterations you make to chip regarding overclocking won't take effect until the Raspberry Pi is rebooted.

Overvoltage Settings

If you are overclocking your Raspberry Pi, you will eventually hit the brick wall past which your device won't go. The precise point at which the Raspberry Pi won't reliably overclock will depend on the individual device due to natural variations in the chip introduced during the manufacturing process. For some users, this limit can be as low as 800MHz while others can find they can push their Pi as high as 1GHz without issue.

The voltage adjustment settings will have upper and lower limits of 8 and -16 which is equivalent to 0.2 V above the stock voltage or 1.4V absolute and 0.4V below the stock voltage or 0.8V absolute. The voltage should be adjusted in whole numbers, and it can't be adjusted below 0.8V (-16) or above 1.4V (8.)

The following settings are accessible from the config.txt file:

- `over_voltage`. It adjusts the ARM's core voltage. The values are given as a whole numbers corresponding to 0.025V above or below the default value of 0 with a lower limit of -16 and an upper limit of 8.

- `over_voltage_sdram`. It adjusts the voltage given to the RAM chip on the Raspberry Pi. As with the over voltage settings, its values are given as a whole number corresponding to 0.025V above or below the stock with a lower limit of -16 and an upper limit of 8.

- `over_voltage_sdram_c`. It adjusts the voltage given to the RAM controller. Its acceptable values are the same as those of over voltage sdram.

- `over_voltage_sdram_i`. It adjusts the voltage given to the memory's I/O system. Its acceptable values are the same as those of over voltage sdram.

- `over_voltage_sdram_p`. It adjusts the voltage given to the memory's physical layer components. Its acceptable values are the same as those of over voltage sdram.

Memory Partitioning

The Raspberry Pi has a single 256 MB memory chip that can be apportioned to the hardware in different ways. The ARM chip is split into two main parts: the general-purpose CPU and the graphics-oriented GPU. Both of these components require memory to work seamlessly, meaning that the 256 MB of memory on the Raspberry Pi should be shared between the two. This partitioning is controlled by a file called "`start.elf`."

The typical split is selected by the maintainers of the Linux distribution installed on the Raspberry Pi. Some select to partition the memory straight down the middle with 128MB being reserved for the CPU and 128 MB being allocated to GPU. This ensures that the graphics hardware can now work at its full potential. Others allow the CPU to have a larger share of memory to increase general-purpose performance.

The majority of Linux distributions include three copies of the "`start.elf`" in addition to the one loaded when the Raspberry Pi boots: "arm128_start.elf", "arm192_start.elf", and "arm224_start.elf." These three files are similar except for one small change: the amount of memory allocated for the ARM's CPU.

Software Settings

In addition to the config.txt file that controls various features of the Raspberry Pi's hardware, there's another vital text file in the "/boot" directory—cmdline.txt—that contains the kernel mode line—options passed to the Linux kernel as the Raspberry Pi boots up.

In a Linux-based desktop, these settings are usually passed to the kernel by a tool known as a bootloader which has its own configuration file. However, on the Raspberry Pi, the options are entered directly into the cmdline.txt to be read by the Pi at boot up. Almost any kernel option supported by Linux can be entered into the cmdline.txt file to change things such as the appearance of the console or the kernel loaded.

Chapter 4: Raspberry Pi's use Cases

Now that you have setup your Raspberry Pi and configured its settings, what next? More specifically, "what can you do with your Raspberry Pi?" As with any PC, here's what you can achieve:

- Using Pi as Home Theatre PC

- Using Pi as a productivity PC

- Using Pi as a web server

- Using Pi to program in Python

Let's dive in and explore these use cases.

#1: Using Pi as a Home Theatre PC

The graphics portion of the ARM's system-on-chip (SoC) design—a Broadcom VideoCore IV module—is capable of full speed HD video playback that uses the popular H.264 format. The chip can also play back audio files in a variety of formats both through the analog 3.5-millimeter audio output and digitally through the HDMI port.

Playing Music at the Console

If you are a developer, you will likely spend most of your time at the Raspberry Pi's console. With the majority of music playback apps aimed at the desktop, it can be a quiet experience even though it doesn't have to be. The Raspberry Pi supports a powerful text-based music playback package called moc (short for music on console). Unlike other tools such as the LXMusic, moc can be installed and used even when there is no GUI on the Raspberry Pi.

To get started, install the moc software package from your distribution's repositories. For the Debian-based Linux distribution, this is as simple as typing the following command at the command prompt of the Terminal:

```
sudo apt-get install moc
```

To load moc, you'll use the command `mocp` rather than `moc`. The reason for using `mocp` is that there is another tool that uses the command `moc`, so a different name is selected to prevent the OS from getting confused between the two software packages.

To get you started, just launch the Terminal and type the following command:

```
mocp
```

The standard `mocp` interface will be split into two panes with the left pane being a file browser that allows you to look for the music to play. The cursor keys will scroll up and down the list, while the Enter key begins playback from the currently highlighted song.

Dedicated HTPC with Rasbmc

Being able to play your music on the Raspberry Pi is one thing, but the ARM chip can do much more. Using its VideoCore IV GPU, Pi can decode and play back full

HD 1080pixels H.264 video, making it a powerful media center machine in a tiny package with incredibly low power consumption.

To get the most from the Raspberry Pi as an HTPC, however, an additional software package is required. This app can be installed in the Debian-based distribution, but there is an easier way to get you started: switching to the Rasbmc distribution.

Rasbmc is distribution aimed specifically at turning the Raspberry Pi into a fully functional media center system complete with video and music playback options, photo viewing and even Internet streaming capabilities. It is based on the popular Xbmc distribution that has been selected by several vendors to power their commercial set-top box systems.

To use Rasbmc, first, download the installer from http://www.raspbmc.com/download/. Installers for Linux OS, OS X, and Windows are usually provided that automatically download the image file for the Rasbmc and write it to the SD card connected to the Pi. When the Rasbmc installer has beencompleted, insert your SD card into the Raspberry Pi and reconnect the power supply making sure your Ethernet cable is connected as well, since Rasbmc needs to download some data from the Web when it first loads.

The initial loading of Rasbmc will take 10 or 15 minutes to complete as it downloads the updates and partitions your SD card, but subsequent loads will be significantly faster. Once you have finished updating, you can now play your favorite music.

#2: Using Pi as Productivity PC

The flexibility of the Pi makes it a perfect choice as a low-power consumption general-purpose desktop computer. Even though it will never reach the same levels of performance that standard desktops provide, its low cost and low power consumption help to make up for any issues with occasionally sluggish performances.

Although the Pi-specific Debian-based distribution provided on the official website doesn't have any of the usual productivity apps you might expect from a general-purpose computer such as a word processor and spreadsheet, this app can be installed using the `apt-get` command.

You can also skip the local installation approach and use cloud-based apps using the Web browser. This can offer improved performance over locally-installed packages at the cost of flexibility and enhanced functionality. Using either a local or cloud-based approach can be used for day-to-day machines for office or school work while not harming the platform's usability for programming and experimentation.

If you are planning to use the Raspberry Pi as a pure productivity PC, it's a good idea to allocate more of the 256 MB of memory for the general-purpose usage and less for the graphics processor using the memory partitioning techniques explained in the previous chapter.

Some of the most popular cloud-based office suites you can use are:

- Google Drive

- Zoho

- Office 365

- Thinkfree Online

Using LibreOffice.org

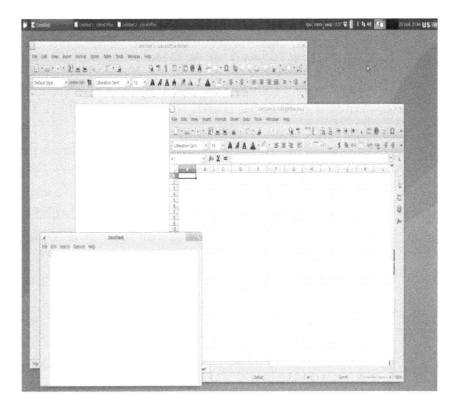

If you don't want to use a cloud-based service, the best alternative would be to install LibreOffice.org. Designed as an open-source and a cross-platform alternative to the popular Microsoft Office suite, LibreOffice.org is powerful and provides just as much functionality as the closed-source Microsoft Office suite.

This functionality would, however, come at a cost. The LibreOffice.org package is huge, taking up almost 400 MB of space on the Raspberry Pi's SD card once all the dependencies have been included. That can be challenging: in its default setup, the recommended Debian-based distribution has a minimal free space available on the SD card compared to what the LibreOffice.org suite requires.

If you want to install LibreOffice.org, you will need a 4 GB or larger SD card. You will also need to resize your root file system to make use of the SD card's available space. For more instructions, you can revisit our previous discussion on Partition Management. Just make sure that you perform this task before continuing with the installation process.

Otherwise, you'll run out of space on your Pi's SD before you can use LibreOffice.org. With enough space on the Pi's SD card, installing OpenOffice.org is not more complex than installing any other software package. Even though it comes bundled with a lot of additional software packages, a single meta-package will take care of everything and installs the software with just a single command.

To install LibreOffice.org on your Pi, open the terminal and type the following command at the prompt:

```
Sudo apt-get install LibreOffice.org
```

When installed, LibreOffice.org will appear as a series of software entries in the Applications Menu in the Raspberry Pi's desktop environment.

These software entries are as follows:

- LibreOffice.org. It is the main application which provides links to the individual sections of the LibreOffice.org suite.

- LibreOffice.org Calc. It is the spreadsheet program equivalent to Microsoft Excel.

- LibreOffice.org Draw. It is a vector illustration program designed for drawing high-quality, scalable pictures for use as clipart in other LibreOffice.org programs.

- LibreOffice.org Impress. It is the presentation program equivalent to Microsoft PowerPoint.

- LibreOffice.org Math. It is a small yet powerful package designed to make it easy to develop and edit scientific formulae and equations for embedding in other LibreOffice.org programs.

- OpenOffice.org Writer. It is the word processor program equivalent to Microsoft Word.

#3: Using Pi as a Web Server

Although the Raspberry Pi is significantly less powerful than most PCs you would find in a data center, this doesn't mean that it cannot be used as a useful server in a home or any business environment. Despite having a small amount of RAM and a relatively underpowered processor, the Raspberry Pi's low power consumption and its silent running make it an excellent choice for serving low-traffic simple web pages to a local area network or even out onto the Web.

It is a fact that a large proportion of modern Web servers execute a combination of Linux, Apache, MySQL, and PHP in what is commonly called the LAMP stack. Linux provides the underlying OS, MySQL database system, Apache the Web server and PHP, a scripting language for dynamic pages. Using an LAMP-based server, you can execute some complex packages that range from CMS's such as WordPress to interactive forums such as phpBB.

All of this is possible with the Pi, yet you won't expect performance similar to that of a powerful commercial server. If you are running the recommended Debian-based distribution for the Raspberry Pi, you will be one-quarter of the way to having a fully-functional

LAMP stack since the Linux portion is already installed.

The next phase is to install the missing components such as Apache, MySQL, and PHP. Type the following at the command prompt:

```
sudo apt-get update
sudo apt-get install php5-mysql mysql-server apache2
php5
```

The above commands will prompt the apt package manager to determine the number of app dependencies required to get a fully-operational LAMP server running. These packages and their dependencies will take up a lot of space on the Raspberry Pi's SD card. Therefore, it is important to partition your SD card before installing the LAMP stack.

Installation of the full LAMP server will take some time to complete on the Raspberry Pi. Don't panic if your system appears to freeze for some time. The installation will continue normally after that. Partway through the installation process, MySQL will prompt you to enter the password. Just ensure that you select a secure password as this will protect your MySQL database.

When the LAMP server stack installation has finished, both MySQL and Apache servers— also known in Linux parlance as daemons—will be running in the background. To verify that the server is working correctly, you can use another computer on the network to connect to your Pi using a Web browser. To do this, just type the IP address of your Raspberry Pi: it will display the default Apache installation page

(See Figure 9-3).

If you aren't sure what IP address the Pi is using, type the following at the command prompt of the Terminal and hit the Enter key:

```
ipconfig
```

Now look out for the IP address listed in the etho section of the window, or the section that corresponds to the network adapter in use on your Raspberry Pi if you are not using the Model B's built-in Ethernet port.

Now that you have successfully installed LAMP stack, what next?

Obviously, you want to begin creating websites. The easiest way to develop and manage websites is by using CMS's such as WordPress (the most popular CMS that powers numerous websites and blogs), Joomla and Drupal.

Wordpress

WordPress is an open-source system that aims to provide users a simple and a powerful platform to generate attractive and interactive websites. WordPress has been built on a base of PHP and JavaScript and provides an attractive Web-based interface that you can use to create rich Internet sites.

Just like the LAMP server, WordPress comes with a selection of software dependencies. You have to ensure that you have around 37 MB of free space on the Raspberry Pi's SD card for full installation, besides the 113 MB required for the LAMP stack.

To install WordPress, launch the Terminal, and enter following command and press the Enter key:

```
sudo apt-get install wordpress
```

If you are sure that you have enough free space, type Y to proceed with the installation process. When WordPress has completed installing, its default installation directory–"/usr/share/wordpress"—should be linked into the "/var/www" directory so that Apache sees the files. Enter the following at the command prompt:

```
sudo ln -s /usr/share/wordpress /var/www/wordpress
```

Next, run the WordPress MySQL configuration script by typing the following command:

```
sudo bash /usr/share/doc/wordpress/examples/setup-
mysql -n wordpress localhost
```

The above code adds a new database into MySQL which has been installed as part of the LAMP stack for WordPress to use. This database will store your posts, user accounts, comments and other details. When this process is complete, you'll be informed to visit http://localhost/wordpress in your browser on the Raspberry Pi so that you can continue the installation.

Fill in the form that will load in your Web browser while picking a descriptive name for your website and setting a secure and memorable password. Be sure to alter the username field from "admin" to something else to make it more secure.

When you complete filling in all the fields, click on "Install WordPress" button at the bottom of the page to proceed with the installation process. The process will take some time (a minute or two). A new Web page confirming the successful installation of WordPress will now load in your browser. To begin using WordPress, just click the "Log In" button at the bottom of the Web page to log into WordPress with the username and password you chose at the earlier screen.

To access WordPress from another computer, you have to create an additional configuration file. This file is created by linking the existing configuration file (set up for the local access) using the following command (in 1 line!):

```
sudo ln -s /etc/wordpress/config-localhost.php
/etc/wordpress/config-ipaddress.php
```

Replace the ipaddress in the above code with the IP address of your Pi. If you have given the Raspberry Pi a hostname in the DNS, you can also develop a configuration file for that hostname using the same command but replacing ipaddress with your chosen hostname. If you don't have a hostname, just use the Raspberry Pi's IP address. For instance, the command for a Pi on IP address 172.168.0.220 would be as follows (in 1 line!):

```
sudo ln -s /etc/wordpress/config-localhost.php
/etc/wordpress/config-172.168.0.220.php
```

#4: Using Pi as a Programming Platform

So far, you've only learned how to use apps that other people have written for Raspberry Pi; but this wasn't the intention of the original. In particular, the chief goal of the Raspberry Pi project was to get people to write their own apps, not just adults, but also kids.

In fact, the Raspberry Pi Foundation has been working around the clock to get the device adopted as an educational toolkit for all age ranges. The key requirement for reaching this goal is ensuring that kids can experience the joy of creating their own apps, instead of just consuming other people's.

Raspberry provides two approaches to achieving this: Scratch and Python. The Scratch programming language was developed by the Lifelong Kindergarten group at the MIT Media Lab in 2006 as an offshoot of the Squeak and Smalltalk programming languages. The Scratch programming language takes the primary concepts of programming and makes them accessible to all. Longwinded typing—tiring and dull for kids—has been replaced with a simple jigsaw-like drag-and-drop programming environment that encourages programmatic thinking among children.

Officially considered as a programming language for ages eight and above, but accessible to even younger programmers with a little help, Scratch is deceptively powerful. Behind its colorful and mouse-driven user interface is a language that has an impressive multimedia functionality.

Encouraging kids to learn how to make their own apps such as games is a great way to sneak some learning into their playtimes. Scratch's friendly user interface and excellent handling of primary concepts means that kids are unlikely to get frustrated by the sudden, steep programming learning curve. Better still, the ideas learned in Scratch provide an excellent foundation for progression to a more flexible programming language such as Python.

Although this section deals with Scratch programming, what I have provided isn't exhaustive. It may also be a little verbose for kids, who want to learn more quickly. More resources about Scratch programming can be obtained at the following URLs:

1. http://info.scratch.mit.edu/support

2. http://info.scratch.mit.edu/WeDo

3. http://www.sparkfun.com/products/10311

4. http://scratch.mit.edu/latest/shared

Python Programming

The Raspberry Pi gets the first half of the name from a long-standing tradition of using fruits to name new computing systems from classic microcomputers such as the Acorn, Apricot and Tangerine to more recognizable modern brands such as Apple and BlackBerry. However, the second half of Raspberry Pi's name comes from Python programming language.

Flexible and powerful, Python was initially conceived in the late 1980s at the National Research Institute of Mathematics and Computer Science by Guido van Rossum as a successor language to the ABC language. Since its launch, Python has grown in popularity thanks to what programmers view as a clear and expressive syntax that was developed with a focus on making sure code is readable.

Python is a high-level language meaning that Python code is written in largely recognizable English language words providing the Raspberry Pi with commands in a manner that is fast to learn and easy to follow. This is in marked contrast to low-level programming languages such as the assemblers which are much closer to how the computer "thinks" but are almost impossible for human beings to follow without experience. The high-level nature and explicit syntax of Python language make it a valuable tool for any programmer who wants to learn the language.

It's also the language recommended by the Raspberry Pi Foundation for those developers looking to progress from the simple Scratch language to more hands-on programming. It has been published under an open-source license platform and is freely available for Linux OS, OS X and even Windows systems. Being cross-platform means that apps written in Python on the Raspberry Pi can be also used on PCs running almost any other OS's.

The only exception will be where the app makes use of Raspberry Pi-specific hardware such as GPIO Ports. If you're a beginner to Python, or even new to programming, you'll find Python modules helpful in developing programs within the shortest time possible. If you're good in C++, you'll find programming in Python to be so simple. This is because the Python code can be wrapped around C++ codes for seamless interaction. By using C++ codes, you'll be in a position to use various tools of C++ without having to understand the language.

Because of its robust nature, Python has been used to develop some of the most popular applications such as Google, Pinterest, Mozilla, SurveyMonkey, SlideShare, YouTube, and Reddit. It is also used to develop games, perform data analysis, control the robot and hardware and create GUIs. This means that several career options demand Python language. Thus, learning Python can be the greatest asset to land that dream job! You may also boost your career with new Python programming skills.

Before we proceed further with Python programming, understanding IDLE is necessary.

Python IDLE

IDLE (Integrated Development and Learning Environment) is an integrated development environment for the Python interpreter. It has been ported to the latest version of Python interpreter. In Linux distributions, it's provided as an optional part of the Python package. IDLE is intended to provide a simple IDE for accelerated development of Python programs. Among the features you'll get:

- Syntax highlighting

- Auto-completion

- Smart indentation

- Integrated debugger with the stepping, persistent breakpoints, and call stack visibility features.

IDLE has two basic types of window: the Shell window and the Editor window. The shell window provides you with capabilities of typing and running the Python codes on the Python shell while the Editor window allows you to capitalize on the IDLE features such as syntax highlighting auto-completion and smart indentation.

IDLE is the default IDE for Python on Raspberry Pi (which means it has already been installed). To begin using IDLE, ensure that it is an updated version. To update IDLE on Raspberry Pi, launch the Terminal and type the following command at the prompt:

```
sudo apt-get install idle3
```

However, if you're not comfortable with IDLE you can try out other text editors such as:

- Emacs. Emacs is a popular text editor that runs on Windows, Mac OS X, Linux and even Android distributions.

- Geany. It is a cross-platform text editor that provides the most basic features of any IDE. It has Python syntax highlighting features such as auto-indentation, even although it doesn't provide auto-deindentation after return and break statements.

- Komodo Edit. Komodo Edit provides the following features: auto-indentation, project and code navigation, code folding, auto-completion, and Snippets.

- SciTE. SciTE is a light, fast and easy to learn text editor, just like the Geany.

- Sublime Text. This has an outstanding selection of powerful features that includes multiple cursors a flexible "goto anything" and a command palette allowing easy access to keyboard features.

Getting started with Python

To get started, you have to understand how to launch the Python app. You can launch Python from the Terminal or use the desktop environment for starting the IDLE app. Simply launch the Terminal and type "idle" at the command prompt. Now that you've launched Python, it's now time to begin coding.

Let's now create our first program in Python. Follow these steps to write your first Python program:

- Open the Python IDLE

- Write the Python language statements (instructions) in the IDLE window

- Run the program

That's it! Isn't it simple?

Now, here's a quick way to see the programming process in action. Proceed and copy/paste the following code into your Python IDLE window.

```
Print ("Hello World! This is my first program")
```

Run the program. What do you see as the output?

Well, the phrase "Hello World! This is my first program" appears.

Congratulations! You've just written your first Python code. At this time, don't worry so much about the meaning of statements. I'll explain the technical details in succeeding sections.

An Overview of Python Application

Now that you have executed your first Python program, what else do you need to know? Well, it's now time to understand the vital components of any Python code including its structure. Python programs have the following structure:

```
import sys
def main ():
    Program statements
```

As you can see from the above program structure, all Python codes should start with the keyword "`import`." Now, what are we importing? The Python programming language is object oriented. Therefore, it has components of all object-oriented programming languages. One such property is inheritance. The ability to inherit features of codes in Python allows programmers to reuse pieces of codes written elsewhere.

Technically speaking, the import statement tells the Python interpreter to declare classes that have already been used in other Python packages without referring to their full package names. For instance, the statement "import sys" informs the interpreter to include all the system libraries such as print whenever the Python program is starting.

What does the statement "`def main ( ):`" mean?

Whenever any Python program is loaded and run, the computer's memory—the Random Access Memory—contains the objects with function definitions. These provide the programmers with the capabilities of instructing the control unit to place the function object into the appropriate section of the computer's memory. In other words, it's like instructing the control unit to check the main memory and initialize the program that needs to be executed.

The function objects in the memory can be specified using names. That's where the statement "`def main ( ):`" comes in. It simply tells the control unit to start executing the Python code statements placed immediately after the statement "def main ( ):"

For example, the Python code below creates a function object and assigns it the name "main":

```
def main ():
    print ("Hello World - ")
    print ("Welcome to Python!"
```

Can you guess what this little program does? If you think, it prints out "Hello World - Welcome to Python!" in the console, you just earned 100 points :-)

In the above code, the Python interpreter will run all the function statements in the Python file by placing the set of functions objects in the memory and linking each of them with the namespace. This will happen when the program is initialized with the import statement.

But more fundamentally, "What are the different elements of Python code?" Well, all Python programs have the following components:

- **Documenting the program.** Any statement in the program (except the first) that starts with "#" is treated as a command line or comment line and will be ignored during execution. This will allow you to comment on sections of the code for proper documentation.

- **Keywords**. The keywords are instructions that the interpreter recognizes and understands. For instance, the word "print" in the earlier program is a keyword. In Python, there are two main types of keywords: the functions and the control keywords. Functions are simply verbs such as print that tell the interpreter what to do while the control keywords control the flow of execution. Examples of keywords are: `and`, `Del`, `from`, `not`, `while`, `as`, `elif`, `global`, `or`, `with`, `assert`, `else`, `if`, `pass`, `break`, `except`, `import`, `print`, `class`, `return`, `def`, `for`, etc. It is a must for you to respect the keywords and not use them as normal names in your Python program.

- ***Modules***. Python program is shipped with a large list of modules that increase its functionality. The modules will help you to organize your code in a manner that's easy to debug and control the code.

- ***Program statements***. The program statements are sentences or instructions that tell the control unit to perform a given operation. Unlike most programming languages, the Python statements don't need a semicolon at the end.

- ***White space***. The white spaces are a collective name that given to tabs, the spaces, and new lines/carriage returns. The Python language is strict on where the white space should be placed in the code.

- **Escape sequences**. The Escape sequences are special characters used for output. For instance: the sequence "\n" in the program tells Python to output on a new line.

Python variables

There's so much that goes on in the main memory of the computer whenever you run a program. Understanding the concept of variables and data types will help you to write efficient programs.

A program—like the one you wrote in the previous chapter—is simply a sequence of instructions (statements) that directs your computer to perform a particular task. For instance, the previous program printed the phrase "Hello World! This is my first program" on the screen when it was executed. But before you could see the output on the screen some data had to be kept in the computer's memory.

The use of data applies to all programming languages—Python included—therefore, understanding the mechanisms of data management in the computer's memory is the first step towards developing robust, efficient and powerful applications.

A variable can be conceived as a temporary storage location in the computer's main memory and specifically the Random Access Memory. This temporary storage location is what will hold the data you would like to use in the program--in other words, the variable location of memory that holds data whenever your program is executing. So, whenever you define a variable, you'll actually be reserving a temporary storage location in the computer's memory.

Now, all the variables that you define must have names and an equivalent data type— a sort of classification of the variable that specifies the type of value the variable should hold. The data types help to specify what sort of mathematical, relational or even logical operations you can apply to the variable without causing an error. Ideally, when you assign variables to data types, you can begin to store numbers, characters, and even constants in the computer's main memory.

Since Python is an oriented programming language, it is not "statically typed." This means that the interpreter regards every variable as an object. Therefore, you have to declare the variables before using them in your program. So, how can you declare variables in Python?

Python variables are usually declared by names or identifiers. Just like any other programming languages you have so far learned, the conventions for naming the variables must strictly be adhered to. Below are some naming conventions that you should follow when declaring variables:

- All variable names should always begin with a letter (A to Z and a to z) or an underscore. For instance, "age" is a valid variable name while "–age" isn't a valid variable name.

- Any variable name you declare cannot start with a number. For instance, 9age is not a valid variable name.

- Special symbols shouldn't be used when declaring variable names. For instance, @name isn't allowed as a variable name.

- The maximum number of characters to use for your variable name shouldn't exceed 255.

To reserve a temporary memory location in the name of a variable, you don't have to use the explicit declaration like other programming languages. If you've had experience in other programming languages such as Pascal or C, I am sure you know that declaring a variable explicitly before assigning any value is a must.

In Python, the declaration of variables usually occurs automatically the moment you assign a value to it. We use the equal sign "=" to assign values to variables. For instance, the statement

```
age=10
```

automatically reserves a temporary storage location in memory space called "`age`" and assigns 10 to it.

It is also possible to assign a single value to several variables simultaneously. For instance, the statement below reserves temporary memory spaces for two variables namely: age and count and assigns them value 30:

```
age, count=30
```

Python language has different categories of data types used to define the storage methods and mathematical operations. Below are examples data types in Python language:

- Numbers

- String

- List

- Tuple

- Dictionary

#1: **Numbers**

The Number data types stores numeric values. The number objects will automatically be initialized whenever you assign a specific value to the variable. For instance, the code illustrated below creates 2 variable objects (age and count) and assigns them the values 10 and 30 respectively:

```
age = 10
count= 30
```

If you want to delete reference to the Number object, you'll use the word "del" followed by the variable name you wish to delete. Consider the code below that deletes two variables: age and count that have already been declared and used."

```
del age, count
```

Python language supports four different categories of number types. These are:

- `int`. when used in a declaration it refers to signed integers. These include those whole numbers ranging from 8 bits to 32 bits.

- `long`. These are long integers. They can be represented either in octal and hexadecimal numbering notation.

- `float`. These are floating real point values. They may range from 8 bits to 64 bits long.

- `complex`. These are complex numbers.

Here is an example Python code using number data types:

```
mynum = 10
print ("The value of the variable mynum is the
following number: %d" % mynum)
```

#2: Strings

Strings are stored as consecutive sets of characters in the computer's memory locations. Python language allows you to use either pair of single or double quotes when defining the strings. Other subsets of string variable types can be specified using the slice operator ([ ] and the [:]) with indexes that range from 0 at the beginning of the string.

The plus (+) operator performs string concatenation (joining of two or more strings) while the asterisk (*) operator performs string repetition. Below is an example of a Python code that uses strings:

```
mystring = "Welcome to Python programming."

# The next statement prints the complete string: "Welcome to
Python programming."
print mystring

# The next statement prints out the first character of
the string:"W"
print mystring [0]

# The next statement prints characters beginning from
the third to the fifth: "lco"
print mystring [2:5]

# The next statement Prints string starting from the
fourth character: "Welcome to Python programming."
print mystring [3:]

# The next statement prints the string two times:
"Welcome to Python programming." "Welcome to Python
programming."
print mystring * 2

# The next statement prints the concatenated string:
"Welcome to Python programming in Python."
print mystring + "in Python"
```

Practical Example: Gaming with Pygame

To illustrate the power of the Python language, this example creates a fully-functional game based on the classic games Snake and Nibbles. To achieve this, we will use an external Python library called `pygame` which is a collection of python modules created to add new functionality of gaming to the Python language.

Although it is possible to write a game in Python without using the pygame module, it's a lot easier to take advantage of the code already written in the pygame library.

To install pygame, enter the following at the command prompt and press the Enter key:

```
sudo apt-get install python-pygame
```

Starting a pygame program is just like starting any other Python project. Open a blank document in IDLE and add the following line to the top:

```
#!/usr/bin/env python
```

Now type the following two lines to import the necessary project modules into your gaming project:

```
import pygame, sys, time, random
from pygame.locals import
```

Obviously, the first line will import the main `pygame` module along with the Python modules `time`, `sys`, and `random`, which we will also use in this program.

Now enter the next two lines in the main window to set up pygame, so it's ready to use in the example program:

```
pygame.init()
myfpsClock = pygame.time.Clock()
```

The first line informs pygame to initialize itself while the second line sets up a new variable called `myfpsClock` that we will use to control the speed of the game. We'll now set up a new pygame display surface (the canvas onto which the in-game objects will be drawn) with the following Python codes:

```
myplaySurface = pygame.display.set_mode((720, 560))
mypygame.display.set_caption("Raspberry Pi Snake
Game")
```

Next up, we will now define some colors for the program. To define the colors, type the following code:

```
myredColour = pygame.Color(255, 0, 0)
myblackColour = pygame.Color(0, 0, 0)
mywhiteColour = pygame.Color(255, 255, 255)
mygreyColour = pygame.Color(150, 150, 150)
```

The next lines of code will now initialize some of the game's variables, so they are ready for use. This is a vital step because if these variables are blank when the game begins, then Python won't know what to do.

```
mysnakePosition = [100,100]
mysnakeSegments = [[100,100],[80,100],[60,100]]
myraspberryPosition = [300,300]
myraspberrySpawned = 1
mydirection = "right"
changeDirection = mydirection
```

Note that three of the variables (`mysnakePosition`, `mysnakeSegments`, and `myraspberryPosition`) have all been set to a list of comma-separated values.

Next, we'll now define a new function that can be called upon later in the program. Type the following lines of code to define the `gameOver` function:

```
def gameOver():
    gameOverFont = pygame.font.Font("freesansbold.ttf", 66)
    gameOverSurf = gameOverFont.render("Game Over", True,
        greyColour)
    gameOverRect = gameOverSurf.get_rect()
    gameOverRect.midtop = (400, 10)
    playSurface.blit(gameOverSurf, gameOverRect)
    pygame.display.flip()
    time.sleep(10)
    pygame.quit()
    sys.exit()
```

Since we now have our code, let us make the snake to move and grow. Type the following lines of code:

```
playSurface.fill(myblackColour)

for position in snakeSegments:
```

```
  pygame.draw.rect(playSurface,mywhiteColour,Rect
(position[0],
     position[10], 20, 20))
  pygame.draw.rect(playSurface,myredColour,Rect(
     raspberryPosition[0], raspberryPosition[1], 30, 30))
  pygame.display.flip()
```

Hopefully, this section has provided you a taste of what you can get with Python. There are many resources out there you can use to learn Python language. Some can be found at the following URLs:

1. http://wiki.python.org/moin/BeginnersGuide

2. http://www.learnpython.org/

3. http://learnpythonthehardway.org/

4. http://www.diveintopython.net/

5. http://wiki.python.org/moin/LocalUserGroups

6. http://wiki.python.org/moin/LocalUserGroups

Conclusion

As you've seen in this book, the Raspberry Pi is more than just a teaching tool for encouraging kids to learn and enjoy programming. It is being applied across a horde of industries from smartphones to IoT with impressive commercial success stories that are unprecedented.

Obviously, you can't paint a landscape without learning its basics. And the fact that you've read the entire book means that you're really interested in Raspberry Pi. Otherwise, if you were not, you wouldn't have read all the pages. Now, this is only the first step. Remember, you want to be a top-notch Raspberry programmer.

Top-notch programmers don't give up along the way. Go ahead and practice to conceptualize all the ideas you have learned in this book. Remember, the rule of thumb in learning - Raspberry Pi included - is practice; and undoubtedly: Good practice makes perfect.

I'm also glad you chose the Raspberry Pi. There's no doubt about the power of it. With the concepts you have learned, you should now be in a position to begin using Raspberry Pi.

Also, if you enjoyed reading this book, *I'd like to kindly ask you for your support by leaving a review on Amazon.* It would be highly appreciated!